UNGRATEFUL CITIZEN

GENE EARL BRADFORD

PROLOGUE

WHEN I RECEIVED an official reply from our White House, I found President Donald J. Trump's response to be precious and elegant. I sincerely hope you will elevate your minds to cherish his message of unity.

Should you manifest wounds of an ungrateful citizen, laced with jealousy, hatred and revenge; I encourage you to reconsider your position so you may heal in the best interest of our country.

Temptation to resist or rebuff the President's theme confirms that people do not handle losing well, and still suffer from mental shock that President Trump remains the leader of these United States of America.

We just witnessed the greatest political upset in history.

Displaying fierce fortitude and the wisdom to stifle various plots to end his tenure, the President has shown he is a worthy knight ready to rule the American Kingdom. Rise up, you mighty patriots, and safeguard the oval office with your powerful vote.

Our Commander in Chief must have the opportunity to execute his agenda and mission while at work, without constant betrayal from the general public, news, media, Democrats, and traitors in the Republican Party. Remember, Rome's demise started with hardened disputes and a gang murder on the Senate floor. Patriotism is the antidote needed to keep our nation supreme.

Book Formatting and Editing by:

Tactical 16 Self-Publishing

A Division of Tactical 16, LLC.

Monument, Colorado

God Bless America.

INTRODUCTION

Upon receiving an official reply from our White House, the moment had arrived to unveil my fresh book titled *Ungrateful Citizen*.

THE WHITE HOUSE G
WASHINGTON

Thank you for your kind words and thoughtful gift. Melania and I deeply appreciate your support. We are honored to serve a country that we love and to work every day to improve the lives of the American people.

Your encouragement, and that of millions of Americans, sustains us each step of the way. By working together, we will deliver on the promise of America for all of our people. We will strengthen our national spirit and ensure that America continues to shine as a beacon of freedom for all the world to see.

We are grateful for your generous gift and support.

God Bless America,

1

VETERAN'S PLEDGE

MISINFORMATION AND PROPAGANDA have painted a dark and gloomy picture that America is a racist domain ready to self-destruct. Contrary to this belief, people have forgotten we reside on a great land that is prosperous, offers many freedoms, and features a strong military poised to protect our borders day or night against all external and internal threats.

I find it necessary to comment on our present state of affairs. Before I go there, two events molded our country from the beginning. First, the American colonies created this nation when they defeated the British crown. Secondly, the confederacy over a four year period from 1861-1865 was winning the civil conflict when a decision was made to allow slaves to fight for their future. Escaping the Willie Lynch Doctrine, slaves migrated north to Yankee strongholds to join a nest of free brothers.

Teamwork on the battlefield proved slaves and white union soldiers turned the tide of war with a triumphant celebration over General Robert Lee and his southern army. Both military actions were a scene of extreme hate and prejudice.

After displaying bravery and true grit during the brawl, slaves became black veterans—earning their own regiment known as the 94th Massachusetts. White infantry surviving the dispute paid tribute to the men of color. For the first time, black troopers slayed white counterparts while avoiding Lynching picnics on a Sunday afternoon.

Dancing in the sky, the colors red, white and blue remind us the national flag clearly unites the fifty states. Any wishful imagination to demolish our democracy will never happen. Our people's loyalty to the stripes assures this prophecy.

A call to duty trespassed my thoughts, inspiring me to enlist in the Marines. While standing on the scales the medical examiner observed my feet were flat and departed the room. I could hear a debate concerning my foot condition. Suddenly, an officer stepped in the space and asked a question. Do you want to serve your country? My response was a gesture: "yes." Just like that I was dispatched to San Diego, California for Boot Camp.

Failure to qualify for military duty would have crushed me mentally. Sparta, an ancient Greek State, threw their rejects in a hole if they were found not worthy of being an Elite Spartan Warrior. In my mind, to take the Oath was truly an honor and I was ripe and ready to protect and defend our American principles against all foreign and domestic enemies.

Military archives will disclose I mimic. The tradition of the 94th Massachusetts, Buffalo soldiers, and the Tuskegee airmen. Unfortunately, citizens with multiple grievances and who have not taken the pledge ignite turmoil and unrest in our cities.

Lambert airport was in plain view as arriving and departing flights took turns touching the concrete runway. Sitting aboard a commercial aircraft the plane began to taxi for takeoff. The seatbelt lights warned passengers to strap tight—the journey was underway.

Four hours later, touchdown guided the recruits to a single green bus. We were curious about our unusual surroundings, as military activity could be seen adjacent to the airport. High expectations loomed large for us all as the colony anticipated an unknown agenda designed to infuse us for combat operations.

At last, the yellow footprints were visible, signaling the end of civilian culture. Orders were shouted to cover a set of imprints. We were rushed into the barbershop and our heads were stripped naked. Uniforms and equipment were distributed as if we were components on an assembly line. Sleeping quarters were overrun on the hot summer night that wrapped up a long and tedious day.

Unwelcome invaders breached our peaceful abode, bearing flashlights with the intent to flog a fellow marine. I recalled this scene from prison movies. Insulted, I leapt from my top bunk and challenged the leader. A squad of fourteen men occupied the building. Collectively, we were from the hoods of Detroit, Chicago, and St. Louis. Speaking with outrage, I stated "Jim Crow is dead!" Drill instructors heard the ruckus and spoiled the blanket party by sending the ghosts from the past to the exit.

The next morning, I was summoned to the office. The platoon was given to me and the marines eradicated an ugly racial incident. Leadership skills were revealed in The Book Art of War, enabling me to create high morale among the rank and file: be fair and seek equal representation. Whites, blacks, and Hispanics were all promoted to squad leaders, and the plan was to flourish.

All competitive honors were kidnapped by the First Battalion as we out-dueled both the second and third battalions. By now, my name floated across the boot camp, tempting drill instructors to arrange a track meet showcasing the platoon leaders. I was in the best shape of my life when I located my lane. I heard a deafening sound as I flashed, to the roars of my comrades in the 1073 series. I had won their respect. However, there was one person deserving higher praise. He was the company Honorman and the heartbeat of the marines.

Graduation day was close as tailors chalked our dress blues and winter attire. The uniform of the day was green, with a starch shirt and trousers. The parade grounds reflected us, the final product and the might of a great powerhouse. Our group of young marines had the stature of an Oscar Image Awards. Branded for life, I would leave boot camp without shooting badges. A furlough was desperately needed at this juncture in my military career, as I yearned for family and friends.

Coming home was a delight. Hugs, kisses, and handshakes accosted me. Conversations, beer and food engulfed my stay for one week and rejuvenated a craving to correct some unfinished business over shooting badges.

Camp Pendleton was my next duty station, and the Marine Corps promptly scheduled a shooting debut. On a Friday morning, I engaged in a solo act. You could hear black crows chatting around 0900 as gunfire shaped tight groups with both pistol and rifle. The range officer stated, "good shooting, marine" and dispensed to me sharp shooter badges for qualifying with 45-caliber pistol and an M-16 rifle.

Perhaps the week of rest prepared me for this challenge, or a grave error was made at the boot camp firing range. Now, I felt complete—full of zeal and eager to tackle new adventures at this enormous training base. War games for Vietnam and Middle East intervention took place during my time there. Identifying booby traps, trip wire, launching rockets, and throwing grenades kept us busy. Hand-to-hand combat lessons was a reality check. If you found yourself face to face with the enemy, you must kill or be killed. Setting day and night ambushes on roads completed our military exercises at Camp Pendleton.

Startling for me, I received paperwork directing me to sea duty school —with my primary mission to enforce Marine and Navy regulations on land and sea. My high test score from the basic written examination provided this unique opportunity. Within the blink of an eye, Navy traditions came knocking. Commanders of US Navy commuted to sea school to select their personal drivers and body guards. A three-star rear Admiral and Commander of the Seventh Fleet chose me to be his orderly. He was the highest ranking officer on the panel and commanded the U.S.S. Coral Sea. This aircraft carrier cruised with golden anchors, showing the world it was legendary.

Navy Royalty reciprocated to their military hardware after the sentry positions were filled. Once again, I was isolated from the group when deployed to Vietnam territory. Treated like a secret package, I was airborne to Manila, Philippines and put on a helicopter seeking a landing pad atop the U.S.S. Pyro, an ammunition ship. This war barge supplied large gun shells for tanks and big guns near the gulf of Tonkin, off the coast of Vietnam. My layover would be short. Soon the pyro would rendezvous with the Coral Sea, thrusting me aboard its shipboard.

From the Pyro portside to the Coral Sea starboard, a zip line stretched a confluence link between ships. I was placed in a cage and pushed to the other side. Halfway through the ride the container dipped below sea level. In disbelief, I contemplated that my life was over, but a jerky recoil lifted my posterior from the water.

The marine detachment awaited my entrance and quickly labeled me section leader. My duties and responsibilities were equal to platoon leader in boot camp. All of my other time was committed to sentinel work, shielding the commodore. When I was off duty, another Marine completed the 24 hour cycle. On deck you could hear pilots inflicting hostile actions in the jungles of Vietnam. Planes backtracked to us for more ordinance to conclude the mission. This pattern would continue until another carrier relieved us for leisure time in foreign ports based in the Far East. Japan; Hong Kong; Subic Bay, Philippines--all were eye-opening ventures. Each ally was styled after the American business model, forcing me to comprehend that the continent I was willing to die for was the greatest alliance on the planet. Until you leave the homeland and observe other lands customs or cultures you will never value the blessings of the United States of America.

Sometimes our planes could not fly in bad weather, as I well remember the sea imploding and threatening to flip ships belly up. Peace and calm was the norm on any given day. These were my Sinbad moments—reminiscing whales playing with their offspring, Russian planes flying close to our battle group, anticipating all-star days when top gun pilots frequented aerial dynamics and would show off combat skills that kept the crew amused.

When activities were slow, I donned the boxing gloves and fought in smokers to amuse the unit. Medical records compiled will provide I injured my left shoulder in a bout. Surgery on the left shoulder was rendered at cubic point hospital. A monkey came to my bed daily as I healed in a woody area. Somehow, the primate understood my fruit was available for him to chew. Ninety days later, I was discharged from the Philippines medical facility to full duty.

Life on the flat deck was pleasant. Uncle Sam made sure that our personnel feasted on the best of food. My favorite dish was the 36-ounce steak with french fries. Movies owned the evening hours until our sleepy eyes shut down.

On a new day the intercom conveyed "man overboard." As a first responder, I joined two sailors in an inflated raft. My mission was to shoot sharks. The search ceased after one hour; the pilot remains were never found. It was past practice for planes to malfunction on takeoff and plunge into the sea.

Repeating a second tour of the Vietnam campaign, my squad would hop its last helicopter flight. Spotted in the rice fields were Vietnamese hard at work. Dressed in black garments and non-LA you could not tell the men from the women. Rules of engagement were in full effect. Silence froze us as we waited for gunfire to penetrate the light weighted machine. Hanging on my body were four magazines as I wondered, would the ammo outlast a gun scrimmage?

A panorama divulged no panic or fear on the ground. Weapons were not drawn. Only then did we realize that the peasants were friendly. A year later the war ended, on April 30, 1975.

Reflections of my Homeland came to mind. The pulse of America was in disarray in the early years of the Vietnam war. Acrimony plagued the sixties. Assassination of our leaders ran rampant. The general population sympathized with a foreign adversary and slammed the Vietnam veterans as baby killers. There can be no denial that America has a track record of unpredictable behavior and judgment.

My speculation on the madness is simple. Cowards burned draft cards and lit fires to galvanize protesters, bashing the war to secrete their shame and disgrace. Fast forward to now, copycat civilians elect not to serve our federation, but engage in rhetoric to undermine and corrupt our republic.

Brave veterans spilled their blood to develop this huge mass from the Atlantic Coast to the Pacific shores. They included Presidents George Washington, Thomas Jefferson, Andrew Jackson, and James Polk. Past lessons have proven that it will take such men and women to guard our nationalism, repelling every imminent danger that will subvert the populace. Treasure your freedom and venerate the fallen on memory day.

2

———————

SHAKE UP

UNABLE TO ACCEPT the outcome of the 2016 election, the Democrats, news media, and the liberal audience still suffer from the mental shock that President Donald Trump captured the White House.

In a desperate effort to redeem themselves, a conspiracy was hatched to dethrone the President by any means necessary. They spread false gossip: first, that Trump did not win the popular vote, and secondly, that Trump supporters are a small base. Hours have been spent guessing what our numbers could be. Some say fifty-three million strong; I say double this tally.

The people have spoken, and I warn the voters to stay vigilant and safeguard the White House.

Bible sermons teach us that Jesus Christ was crucified. What was strange on that day was that the crowd surveyed the spectacle and lacked the courage to rescue the Messiah. We, as Americans, cannot imitate this cowardly inaction. Rise up and keep the President in the oval office for a second term. He is a reliable knight.

Who among you could have withstood the onslaught thrown at our sitting President? Jousting with the Commander in Chief every day and every minute has propelled Trump forward unchained. He refuses to be a puppet for the wicked news outlets, liberals, and Democrats.

This disgruntled cluster does not understand their roles; they are not the President. He did not authorize you to speak on his behalf. Trump holds this prestigious honor and needs only the public trust to propagate an unprecedented strategy.

Making a chess move, I placed forever stamps on a package and dropped it in the mail. To my amazement, I received a prompt reply from the White House. It gives me joy to share the precious and elegant language of the President of these United States with you. Posted in the introduction of this masterpiece, I provide comfort for your digestion. Many of you do not know the President in this way. You judged him based on what you heard from a fearful segment of our society.

Attacking the President with negative nouns, verbs, and modifiers is an assault on all Trump advocates. We welcome his tweets. Clear communication is paramount. No President before him took advantage of this new technology.

To complete the communication process, every citizen must look in the mirror and inspect themselves. Some of you won't like what you discover. So how can you give a fair and objective assessment of the President? By now, you should have concluded Trump is not a racist as people claim. To insist he sheds light, that it takes a racist to define hatred. Often the race card is played when bitter souls get frustrated with their inner self. This emotional tactic will not keep Trump from grasping a second term in office.

I sincerely hope that you permit this message to knead your mind, because this is the antidote needed to heal our nation from the mental shock that occurs when we witness a massive political upset. Folklore will tell that Trump was the undisputed political champion who caused a shakeup that changed America's status on the world stage.

Elated, the President gets a Gold Star in my book as he tries to recruit other world leaders to shine as well. A rainbow coalition is positioned to calibrate screens and cards in upcoming elections. I predict the Nobel Peace Prize will be hoisted on the White House lawn shortly.

Left no choice, I stand with President Trump on the National Anthem issue. This topic was the centerpiece that triggered feedback from the snow mansion. Professional football players kneeling at our flag is unacceptable conduct! No minority group will dictate terms concerning the emblem. We lost too many lives in battle to settle for a frail uproar. Soldiers are willing to die for their country, while athletes play a game with a running time clock. We are the home of the brave—who birthed this empire in the American Revolutionary War with the American flag leading the way. As a military veteran, I did not risk my life so that football players can bend their legs in dishonor. They get paid to entertain.

As a Little League football legend, my dynasty flew the American flag with our colors of black and gold. We won six super bowls and three national championships. The NFL's Jacksonville Jaguars drafted one of our players at the cornerback slot. Stooping down on the flag then was never an option. We stood in victory. Our record was 59-3-1. We were undefeated champions in the state of Missouri for six years.

Championship teams at any level must be a class act. The Alabama Crimson Tide is an excellent example of proper ethics when visiting the President. The Tide even prayed with Trump, transmitting their tenacity to continue valuable work.

Revoking invites from defiant teams was the right move by Trump. I am confident the Washington Capitals will be the next class act, accepting White House invitations and maintaining tradition. I've already purchased my tuxedo trimmed with red socks and bow tie, hoping I'll get a memo stating, "you're the next luxurious guest."

Police related shootings are a secondary topic, and I will give facts in my third chapter, Double Talk. As for now, NFL owners have ruled that players must stand at games or face punitive fines. The policy is in writing. Players follow instructions and do not inflame strife. There is a secret recipe for all internal threats that test our resolve.

Breaking news once again agitates dissent on the borders. The national security of this nation trumps all other matters, including migrant children. The law clearly states you can seek entry to America by going through the proper channels. As a taxpayer, I want to know my next-door neighbor. If you are a refugee crossing the river to escape crime, do not expect mercy from the United States when your actions violate immigration statues. We are not obligated to shelter you. Crime plagues America, but there is no exodus to vacate the States for third world landscapes.

The appropriate remedy for separating two thousand children from their parents is to send them back to Mexico. The Mexican government must be held accountable for taking care of its people. It must provide them jobs, homes, better living conditions, and curtail crime for migrants.

President Trump signed an executive order to keep children with parents, because Congress is pathetic. Traitor Republicans and stone-faced Democrats are unfit to propose a bill that sponsors a security wall. It is common knowledge that open terrain is vulnerable to an invasion. Yet, they cannot fathom the idea of the President receiving credit for this milestone.

While in college, I studied the three branches of government. The executive branch gives the President the power and authority to enforce the law. Secondly, the legislative branch makes the law; this body is not doing its job. Lack of perspective has made the President's plan challenging to achieve. Finally, the judicial branch interprets the law, and bewilderment stimulates this section of the government. The news circuit is the mouthpiece for the judicial arm, activating volcanic eruptions in the streets with menacing protesters defying the President's policies.

I doubt very seriously that the general population has to siphon the above knowledge. Trump will repeat as President via the common sense vote. Voting with empathy is fragile and will be the rash to stifle the Democrat's electorate.

Exaggeration of the treatment given to children in the holding pen is done by design. I toiled as a state employee at a youth facility on a Thursday afternoon. Two teenage boys began arguing over a girl. One kid pulled a butcher knife and charged. I was standing near the dining room, and the weapon was taken from the assailant as he passed. A report was made of the incident. The state reacted with an investigation for abuse of a minor.

Retorting at the interview, I told them that a life was saved that night. If I had not acted and taken action, a child would be dead. The board dropped the case! The point is, do not be mislead by television sound bites of children crying and begging for their parents' presence in federal centers. Basic standards are being met in federal and state housing. Food, shelter, recreation, and toilets are available to accommodate both boys and girls. That the staff does care about the welfare of children is a reputation that is underserving and untrue. Tainting this image is part of of the Democrats' political party goal to retake the White House.

3

———————

DOUBLE TALK

FLASHING lights racing over streets in urban centers alert the community that police officers are busy at work. Often their services are not appreciated. Delivering babies, directing traffic, confronting dangerous criminals, and monitoring protesters when they decide to become a violent mob are just a few assignments implemented in a day's shift.

Seeds of this occupation were planted in elementary school when I entered the patrol program. Our leader was a math teacher who actually held court to hear cases concerning student affairs. Dressed in crisp blue jeans, a blue jacket, and a white chest belt, we were primed for duty.

There was a sense of pride among us as we reported school violations such as fighting, stealing, gambling, and smoking cigarettes to the principal network. At an early age, I learned a code does exist within a group to stick together when outsiders resent safety control and rule enforcement.

Visions of being in law enforcement would lead me to Langley, Virginia, for possible employment. I was on the wires for six hours, taking a polygraph test. Upon conclusion of the interrogation, I received the red circle and was told not to make trouble by filing a civil rights or EEO complaint. As I was turning sixty-eight years old, a retirement booklet was completed after thirty-six years of dedicated workmanship with another government agency.

On my way out to pasture, my family and country must know: I tried to reach the highest echelon in our government. If given a chance, I most likely would have retired from the agency. I am a U.S. Marine and was trained to accomplish my mission.

While visiting the Gateway City at a local Boys and Girls Club, President Ronald Reagan was aware of my endeavors. I left my Kiddie Patrol behind to aid in Internal Security for the President. On this day, the recreation center resembled a military base. Emulating the readiness of the Marines, they were erect and in place for the big moment. Organizing the patrol was an idea to encourage youth not to destroy or deface the new structure and let the business council know we appreciated their sponsorship to make the club a reality. The Grand Opening ceremony recorded the patrol's first official action.

Seeking higher education in the law enforcement field, I graduated with a Bachelor in Science Degree in Administration of Justice with a 3.5 GPA, annexing my military experience enforcing Marine and Navy regulations; I interacted with people daily without any shots fired over a four year period.

At this point, I hungered to spiel the double talk that overcasts police shootings in our inner cities. A swinging pendulum cannot regulate police encounters in our zip codes. Who lives and who dies is distinguished by fate. This equation is complexly unfurling a negative vibe between the police, citizens, and criminal suspects.

Pockets of the metro zone hope for a magical outcome of removing their kin from the coroner's body bag collection.

Select any city limits resembling St. Louis, Chicago, Detroit, Memphis, Kansas City, and others: this storyline is common. Crime is an epidemic contaminating our natural habitat and spreading a stream of cancerous sores. Even though funeral chapels and crime labs leak evidence, the police are wanted to restore law and order so we all can breathe easily.

Blindfolded, the general public have gotten their sentiments tangled. Staying quiet about the above narrative and acting out when the police put down violence is hypercritical. Being quick to protest and burn property without facts is foolish conduct. Ignoring police officers slain in the line of duty does not heal the Black Lives Matter movement. There is plenty of sympathy for both sides.

City grids—prepare yourselves. The police will dominate and own the streets. Floating through the grapevine are illicit rumors. Are the police frightened, or criminals? Should you decide to test this myth, be aware: a prison or grave awaits your entrance.

Whites, blacks, Native Americans, Mexicans, and other races have engaged in brutal murders against each other. It's the nature of the beast. This mayhem and hatred represents only a small percentage of the total population. The majority of your countrymen strive to live in harmony and peace, as America makes its bid to be great once more.

However, losing a loved one is a terrible stressor. Visuals honoring the death of family blood are plentiful. Demands from families for the police to solve the crimes have risen. Yet, these voices cry out for the police to be held accountable when they are involved in police shootings. Meaning they thirst for police to lose their jobs and go to jail. This is double talk in its purest form. The public cannot straddle the fence. You must choose to enhance the police if you want them to risk their lives and guard the metropolis.

Shifting focus, I would like to pierce the fog surrounding the police culture. There is no doubt that corruption flows in police precincts. Exposure to this behavior will eventually come to light for justice. Protesters will also pay a heavy price for trespassing the nation's interstates, destroying property, and harassing decent fans at various sports venues. Protecting the safety of Americans is a necessity during times of unrest. A crackdown is forthcoming. A rabble must be repressed. The protesters' purpose is to strain law enforcement resources and interrupt business in malls, creating a loss of profit. Two can play this game. The government must levy punitive fines against agitators jumping to conclusions and rushing to judgment without facts. We have a court system in motion to address any criminal complaint. Sublet the process to take its course.

On August 12, 2018, twelve months after the Charlottesville melee, counter-protesters used the excuse of reverence for a single death to steal the spotlight from southerners who rallied to preserve the Robert E. Lee monument. The Civil War was an unforgettable saga. Nobody has the right to abolish southern annals. To do so will dismiss the feat of black slaves who won their freedom in the trenches, and banished the slave industry from American soil. Excited and proud, President Abraham Lincoln signed the Emancipation Proclamation on January 1, 1863, making enslaved Americans free.

Congress promptly modified the U.S. Constitution to benefit formal slaves. It was prosperous times from 1863 to 1877, establishing the Reconstruction period. The American dream was visible for the South to pacify. Many blacks held seats on the hill, purchased homes and cars, owned deeds to land and livestock; science, education, and the arts were taught in schools.

A trio of Civil War Amendments made the above transparent. The Thirteenth Amendment abolished slavery in 1865. The Fourteenth Amendment provided equal protection under the law in 1866. Finally, the Fifteenth Amendment in 1970 granted voting rights regardless of previous conditions of slavery, race, or color of a person's skin. Federal troops were stationed all over the South until the Republican party abandoned the fight for racial equality and black rights. The Reconstruction experiment vanished in 1877 with no military protection.

President Trump was exact in his understanding of events in Charlottesville. Both sides had bad and good henchmen eager to entangle in hatred. Law enforcement did a superb job of preventing blood stains from coloring the park grounds. Graphics exposed the helmets, shields, sticks, pipes, and masks: each camp's weapons of choice.

Be wary counter-protesters; marching with portable lanterns on August 12, 2017, was just a warning! Leave Robert E. Lee shrines alone. Stone pillars will not bite you, and you can't shake people to denounce and bury war chronicles. Slavery ended officially on June 19, 1865.

During the 16th and 19th centuries, the Trans-Atlantic slave trade routes began in the ports of West Africa, the Caribbean Islands, American and European colonies. This was the world order at the time. Countries do not owe people of color and apology for conducting business as usual. All through history, losing on the battlefield sealed the fate of a conquered people. Thank God that America did some soul cleaning and discerned a civil war would exterminate the slave trade.

There was no discrimination amidst societies. Romans, Africans, Native Americans, and Europeans were all slaves at one time. Each dynasty has tales of slave revolts trying to topple the savage enterprise. Three civilizations plundered Africa's northern horn and impacted the world through procreation, seizing treasures, and natural resources. Concubines were the lifeline that kept the ruling monarchs afloat. Healthy birth rates supplied both the military ranks and working hands to harvest the various crops. Civil war clashes were constant amid the Moors, Romans, and Viking Kingdoms. Hungry for conquests, racism evolved from shedding the enemy blood. This catalyst exists today and runs freely in our veins to inflict hate crimes against humanity.

Police safety is the buffer desired in the line of work. Miniature racing drones can be released from car bulb cases twenty yards before chasing cars or responding to domestic dispute calls. The goal is to prevent element of surprise shootings. Drones can search for dangerous weapons and alert officers if their lives are in danger.

Cease the pattern of walking towards a suspect when exchanging verbal language. Maintain a five-yard distance until you are sure a comfort zone has been established. Too often, officers are found shot with their own guns and stabbed within the limit range.

Take heed: the police must adjust their mindset while conducting patrols on the road. You are not a social worker. There is no time for babysitting grown adults when they find themselves targets of the law. The color of a suspect's skin is irrelevant when a crime has been committed. All humans bleed cherry red when the flesh is pierced.

A person busy elsewhere cannot criticize a policeman when his life is in peril. After all, you might be the next suspect trapped in the web of crime. What is your decision with an episode confronting law enforcement officials? A tip for the prudent: regard the law, and you will live another day.

4

MIDTERM LOTTERY VOTE

ON NOVEMBER 6, 2018, I was first in line at the polls to cast my vote for the Republican ballot. I've been harping in this writing how the Democrats miscalculated red votes. A split decision in the halls of Congress is history. The house was a Christmas gift to Democrats. Renegade Republicans either affected or died with the notion of cleansing the White House, giving easy passage to vacated seats. Don't be astonished that a few turncoats will oppose Trump in 2020. One hundred million people participated in the course, setting a record for voter turnout.

Meanwhile, the Democrats are making a last stand to dismiss Trump from office with their victory. After this hostile takeover plummets, there will be an assassination plot on Trump's life. The news media will set the tone for unforeseen savagery. Constant headlines rousing an overthrow of the oval office will be the spark. Before unknown assassins get started, hear my words! President Trump is a beloved man. America will not tolerate or condone such evil intentions. Remember the Alamo, America—and find the mettle to safeguard the President while he is serving this great nation.

Did you take notice that a reporter feigned his death for one year, and the media blamed President Putin as the culprit? Not once did the American Congress apologize to Putin fort their fallacious allegations. This round, the Saudi King is accused of plotting the death of another newsman. In this instance, the President has used sound judgment by waiting to get all facts before condemning a world leader for a murder he did not sanction.

Waging war on global heads of state seems to be commonplace with the free press. I always believed the mission of a journalist was to be a fair and objective voice. Plenty of headlines reflect opinions, assumptions, and accusations without attestation. President Trump tagged the falsehood fake news, and I concur. Our President has worked very hard on behalf of the American people. Let's review together his performance up to the midterm lottery pick and give him a grade. Based on the below report card, I give him and the First Lady an A-plus for their outstanding service to the United States of America.

1. Endorsed tax reform
2. Endorsed criminal justice reform
3. Enlightened and educated the country on corruption in the halls of Congress
4. Exposed leaks in the White House
5. Forced traitors to leave the White House
6. Banned bump stocks to shun massive shootings
7. Encouraged new trade deal with countries
8. Reopened closed plants in America
9. Responsible for a booming economy
10. Responsible for the low unemployment rate
11. Appointed two Supreme Court Justices
12. Established a space unit using military personnel
13. Vetted terrorists crossing borders

14. Rebuilt our military with new logistics, technology, and supplies
15. Authorized FEMA to aid all Americans who experience natural disasters such as wildfires, hurricanes, tornadoes, flooding, and volcanic eruptions
16. Blamed both left and right protesters for Charlottesville unrest
17. Improved the Veteran's Administration Center
18. Commanded the defeat of the ISIS threat
19. Negotiated the release of Veteran remains in North Korea
20. Influenced North Korea to ceasefire missile barrage
21. Denied Russian collusion in the 2016 election
22. Ordered Homeland Security to protect our southern borders
23. Restored America's image on the world stage
24. Hosted the Bush family on White House grounds as they mourned President George H.W. Bush
25. Stimulated stock market growth
26. Engaged China in a tariff war
27. Authorized government shut down over border wall funding
28. Bargained for the release of U.S. citizens who were prisoners in China
29. Revamped the intel community
30. Battled news media and critics in a war of words
31. Stocked our judge seats throughout the court system
32. Sought health care for the nation
33. Responsible for low fuel prices
34. Pushed for law and order to fight crime in the streets of America
35. Communicated with world leaders for peace and autonomy
36. Enforced immigration policy
37. Enforced national security policy
38. Provided financial aid for farmers affected from trade war

Democrats and the news circus will not open this window for your critique. It's my wish that you judge him with sense. Blinders must be removed so that the truth rays can be seen and sportsmanship displayed after losing in the 2016 presidential election. Circulating that big lie—Russia hacked votes—is ridiculous and insane. I spoke no Russian dialect and was not persuaded by television ads. I think for myself and struck the bell for Trump. Double-dealing aristocrats boldly publish books and mix songs to cripple the pauper's mental make up. Dreams are abandoned. Taking the President's lead, I request to be heard. What is forbidden in this society is insight from plain laymen. Rushing to standby by the Snow Mansion, *Ungrateful Citizen* was created as an aspiration to spike Democrats from blocking and hindering that White House's goals and objectives. I have no taste to do book tours until I know that President Trump has been elected to office for a second term. Unite mighty patriots, and save your nation! One more time, remember the Alamo and the nonbelievers who forsake our savior. His final words were, "Forgive them, for they know not what they do." God gave his approval for President Trump to rule America while angels rejoice in his footsteps! Abstain from being an ungrateful citizen. Should you listen to the division, our realm will crumble.

Today, January 3, 2019, the opening of the 116th Congress bloomed. Freshman candidates swore to serve faithfully. Quickly, these vertebrates began taking swipes at the President with eight tentacles of hell. Trump's feints have kept them at bay for twenty-four months. Feeding off their jealousy, the President is doing a magnificent job; Democrats' body motions went straight to belligerent mode. Eight traps are posted for comprehension:

1. Ungrateful Citizens
2. Media Discredit Crusade
3. Congress Insubordination
4. Border Wall Tiff

5. Russia Investigation
6. Sex Scandals
7. Impeachment
8. Assassination Plot

Young and immature females are slinging profanity at our President, and I urge them all to stay in a matron place. Don't believe the hype that foresees women laying siege in America and making men secondary citizens. This joke is not a laughable comedy. Men have dominated earth from the outset of time and fought each other for supremacy. What makes you believe that we will consent to the opposite sex seducing us with broken heart fables, knowing full well you are not a pure species? Have you forgotten that Eve defied God in the garden?

The plan is set for another female to irritate Trump in the 2020 elections. In the garden of Eden, God favored man over woman. He created her to be man's helpmate, not the leader of the human race. For her defiance, God punished women to painful childbirth; ordained to mesh in intercourse kindled a population explosion.

I am tired of seeing fornication entice women to covet dollars for sexual fun and pleasure. Men who were failing to pay heard screams of rape, sending them to jail. Serving time for some proved to be a mistake. Women confessed they lied about the courtship. Child support fleecing is another tool—rewarding women for sexual satisfaction. Unable to steal rich men's coins, they talked up "the me too movement" to slander and shame powerful men who exploited their feelings. I beg to differ that women are victims. They relish their wild and promiscuous ways.

Words do matter, but there must be powerful testimony before sabotaging a man's career over wet panties. Women do fabricate, murder, abort babies, embezzle, and commit suicide. You are not a stable or innocent lot. Scrutiny must be relevant when listening to tales of immoral conduct.

Over the years, I observed women altering prudence on various topics, and I expect you to do the same in the 2020 primary. You and I know women are attracted to strong men and will not raise their sons to be soft and timid. Escort me as I smoke out all of the ungrateful citizens who reside in our neighborhoods and still suffer from mental shock that President Trump roams the White House gallery.

5

UNGRATEFUL CITIZEN

THE STANDOFF over the border wall showcased that government employees are a selfish work unit. They beg for paychecks when they have seen footage of caravans scattered at our borders, trespassing without permission. With one voice, the entire nation can broker the wall a success story. In unison, we said to Congress, build the wall, and protect the southern border. Promptly, the partial shutdown was over. People returned to work with a sense of pride that they put country before self. You already knew that back pay was forthcoming. I must question, do your eyes ache from infections? Are the images compelling enough to ignore the crisis?

President Trump had border officials lecture America on troubles without the wall. Yet, you rebuffed their pleas. Remaining mute only complicated the Brouhaha. Fear to take action caused financial stress for 800,000 laborers.

The hour has come for the President to declare a National Emergency in the best interest of America. Democrats are a fallen bunch, still nursing fractures from the 2016 defeat. They lack the focus to provide capital for Trump's proposal. I am further frustrated that the opulent society has not stepped up and aided the wall.

Even the middle class and poor could assist by playing a mega lottery to uplift the structure—finally, capture monies from CIA pockets, drug cartels, and oil companies.

In the future, pass bills to freeze Congress' pay when they paralyze our government. In this particular crisis, sovereignty has a task and burden to situate with the President of these United States. He won the election! The discontented will abide by our vote. Trump is anchored in the White House, whether you sanction his presence or not.

Ungrateful Citizen is in full campaign mood. The memoir serves as a wild card that will sway perplexed voters to the Trump Express, speeding to the finish line in the 2020 elections.

Don't forget the President's obligation is to make the nation rudimentary. Let's not discriminate against his bold tactics! Other presidents bared to leap the inferno.

As we are going into recess, my brain seeks soothing. The volume on smooth jazz tunes is heightened. I nudge you to browse these pages with soundtracks in the background; relaxation is instant and boosts comfortable reception. Collectively the tones sum up Trump's legacy, and I request a fair evaluation from you. By now, your aging shell should be cleansed after retaining the beneath hit melodies.

1. "The Journey" Jim Adkins, 2015
2. "State of Mind" Allen Carman, 2018
3. "Let Me" Kenya, 2015
4. "Land of Passion" Hubert Laws, 2002
5. "Getting Better" Monty Steward, 2018
6. "Now or Never" Darryl Williams/Johnathan, 2018
7. "Crossroads" Mel Holder, 2018

8. "Heat" Jazmin Ghent/Philippe Satsse, 2018
9. "Shuffle the Deck" John Novello, 2017
10. "Osaka Cool" Larry Carlton, 1997
11. "Expressway" Walter Beasley, 2010
12. "On and On "Bob Baldwin, 2013

Gripping the remote, I began tapping the channel buttons to find the NFL Championship Game. Intrigue was sprinkled between two overtime thrillers. Grieving over a helmet to helmet miscall, the Saints demonstrated prey cannot appreciate a lethal throbbing. The game was concluded in overtime. The Saints quarterback heaved a dreadful ball downfield for a game-ending interception. The happy Rams ran the leather egg into field goal range and celebrated the kick, spearheading a Super Bowl intrusion.

Unlike the Saints, the Patriots did not sob when their quarterback lofted two interceptions and the defense was blanketed with yellow fabric for fouls. Tucking neat uniforms, the raid crept across the goal line for a ninth Super Bowl excursion. Both tilt-lists sent the vanquished fan base into a frenzy that another Super Bowl eluded them. Defeatism drives people nuts, spawning envy, resistance, and spite.

Inclement weather teased MLK festivity with freezing snowflakes. Churches, basketball tournaments, concerts, and media would not be deterred. Pausing, I reverted to the nonviolent March on Washington, D.C. for freedom and jobs on August 28, 1963—urging modification of America's racial, economic, and civil rights policies. For this action, there was a reaction ejecting a speeding bullet to muffle his words. Still saddened, I miss him dearly and expressed tranquility when his lineage flipped the coin toss at Super Bowl LIII. The extravaganza provided oversight: America has reached the mountain top. Martin Luther King, Jr.'s "I Have A Dream" speech is perpetual and sows seeds vouching my New England Patriots spanked the L.A. Rams with a 10-3 score.

Recovering from the September 11, 2001 aggression, the Patriots rubbed the Super Bowl prize in 2002, reviving America's promise to stamp out tyranny. The Patriots' fidelity continues to energize football fans. It would have been perfect to see the Boston flight leading the military flyover, glorifying Super Bowl LIII and affirming that MLK's dream is alive and thriving.

Two excerpts from his teachable address must be retained. He advised that people must not be guilty of wrongful deeds. Let us not seek to satisfy our thirst for freedom by drinking from the cup of bitterness and hatred. We must forever conduct our struggle on the high plane of dignity and discipline. Noteworthy people cannot walk alone. We must not allow our creative protests to degenerate into physical violence. Our white brothers have realized their destiny of being free is intertwined.

Those who hold the cup of bitterness and hatred agitate racism in this country. Citizens must recognize that freedom prevails. Do your part, and stop being sensitive to piffle remarks.

In 2018 I boarded the Lincoln train to the Big Easy for vacation. I did a pit stop at a Cajun Restaurant outside the city, three miles from the Whitney Plantation. When we arrived fifteen minutes later, we had to wait for a tour guide. The first exhibit detailed the history of slave insurgency. Widespread satires vented slaves were not satisfied with brutal living conditions, thrusting over 500 recorded slave revolts. Except for a few, mastery uprisings were suppressed by local militia and federal troops. One insurrection was singled out for its brutal message. In 1811, the German coast resistance mutilated slaves and mounted heads on poles as a warning—stay in your place, and accept bondage.

Before 1791 the Haitian revolution led by Toussaint Louverture overthrew the French Government, claiming an independent state known as the Republic of Haiti; France sailed home, regretting the

Haitian flag polarizing the red sky. Freedom triumphs are indexed for your absorption.

1. 869, A.D. Zant Rebellion
2. 1570 Gaspar Yagna Rebellion
3. 1730 First Maroon War
4. 1733 St. John Insurrection
5. 1791 Haitian Revolution
6. 1839 Amistad Ship Rebellion
7. 1841 Creole Ship Rebellion, U.S. Coasts

Fading blood drops tantalize the memory cells, for a high price was paid when slaves duelled oppressive regimes. Participants were shot, hung, mutilated, and rotted in prison. World powers have a new global order in place. ISIS is a fading force, in line with past terrorists. The tour escort has returned and beckons my group for a one hour trek.

Valentine's Day ventilated an avalanche of love chocolates, cards, and flowers, stroking hearts and curing wrecked minds. President Trump did the opposite ten hours after midnight, when he handed Congress sugar-free candy declaring a National Emergency. I forecast this stunt earlier in my work and rave that a new Valentine's Day massacre pulverized soft Democrats and traitor Republicans. I am asking America: do not judge the color of the President's skin, but measure the content of his character. He validates invincibility and strength while making a final stance on disputable positions. Personal reflections are descending, suggesting why you must vote the Trump-Pence Ballot in 2020.

- National Security
- Economy
- Immigration Policy
- Law and Order

- Religious Freedom Infrastructure
- Strong Military
- Bogus Probe Against President
- Affordable Health Care
- Rebuke Socialism
- Abortion Laws
- Space Patrol
- Tax Reforms
- Trade War
- Foreign Policy
- Eliminate Green Deal
- Corrupt Congress
- Fake News Media

Republican Party 2020 VOTE
TRUMP-PENCE BALLOT
AMERICAN PATRIOTS

Paper war has manifested court logs. The three branches of government are bickering for power and the infinity of the United States. Only the Supreme Court can convert the White House's insubordination from a sea of ungrateful citizens.

Ides of March anniversary is March 15, 44BC. Unsavory statesmen jabbed Julius Caesar on the Senate floor. Twenty-three wounds penetrated his butchered body, transgressing an incarnation into today's political arena. Congress' dysfunction boils from visualizing President Trump as a modern era Caesar.

Sunday, Sixty Minutes aired an interview with Andrew McCabe confessing to using the 25th Amendment to sweep Trump out of office. Passages in his book are the Nexus that expose the fruit of the poisonous tree. The Copula of FBI Rogue Agents taints the RussiaN Probe. James Comey, Rosenstein, Congress members, the liberal press, and the Mueller investigation are part of the McCabe Farce.

There is no way President Trump could be found guilty of tort charges.

If the upward was Plan A, what was Plan B? Uneasy bureaucrats had no other recourse but to purge Trump, blocking a second term jubilee. Lately, rivals of Trump are whining fears for their safety! Well, you should have gauged repercussions before foiling his presidency. I chose to scribble *Ungrateful Citizen* to voice my disgust with Trump haters. Others elect to use flexible tactics serving omens. We will protect our President against all domestic terrorism.

President George Washington unraveled a scheme to shorten his life on June 28, 1776. In retaliation, he lynched the leader in a public square days before signing the declaration of independence on July 4, 1776.

Previous presidents never got the chance to ostracize evil antagonists. Most perished by a long rifle or handgun. Whether knives or bullets are the weapons of choice, its limpid division of ideas and principles generate murder for sure. Names shared are verification that presidents have a dangerous job just to be hunted by shooters contracted with government and private conspirators.

1. John F. Kennedy; Slayed
2. Abraham Lincoln; Slayed
3. Andrew Jackson; Slayed
4. James A. Garfield; Slayed
5. William Taft; Slayed
6. William McKinley; Slayed
7. Theodore Roosevelt; Botched
8. Ronald Reagan; Botched
9. Donald Trump; Botched

The last escaped a murder endeavor when a British native snatched a policeman firearm to hurt Trump at a local rally on June 18, 2016. The culture of America is vehement and hints at revolution, over what quarrels?

President Trump is the Commander in Chief of the military. It will be up to the combat soldier to keep America free or succumb to socialism. How safe do you think America will be with fingernails hovering over the nuclear button? When you hear the words, I'm hot, and the thermostat is not near, brace yourselves! She will strike that red button, boasting it's my prerogative. Male contenders dream of mocking Trump's status. They will never perpetrate his style and wit.

Worldwide, journalists insist on beating the White House only to find themselves in a bowl of mess. Ninety were found murdered in 2019, 360 detained in multiple countries. President Trump has executive privilege to castigate and vilify the press and private citizens who are dumb enough to curse and slander him. Nice guys finish last on this planet. Respect is a neutral zone that must not be cross if you want Trump loyalists to remain docile. There is no need for a triumphant party to be angry and violent. Trump is our leader. Losers wear the ungrateful citizen's stripes, and cry, threaten, complain, plot, and scream the word "racism" as a fixative to coup the oval office.

Dosing off in black history class, I was interjected in a debate between Booker T. Washington and D.E.B. Dubois. It was a diverse group with a white instructor. Fireworks began early, having both sides screeching the men were Uncle Toms who bilked black people. Raising my hand to be recognized, I requested to speak. Silence captivated the room. First, I illuminated them. We had strayed from the debate question. Who was the best leader during the antebellum epoch? Booker T. Washington had optics that blacks should explore trade jobs using hands as skilled labor to earn wealth in America. D.E.B. Dubois preached that blacks must go the intellectual path and graduate from college. Wisdom would open doors to prosperity in this country.

Secondly, I told them the Uncle Tom myth deserves a hasty interference. Lack of knowledge is like walking earth with frozen eyes, unable to steer a foolish tongue. The Uncle Tom I applaud was a slave hero who was beaten to death by the Legree Plantation owner for not whipping a slave and tattling on two slaves who opened flood gates, marring his crops.

The sellout Uncle Tom was sketched in a novel titled *Uncle Tom's Cabin* composed by Harriet Beecher Stowe, published in 1852. The novel went on to be a best selling piece and stage play. As we were a split nation at the time, reviews were feral. The North embellished its literature, and the South had a bland portrayal of the slave system. Slave revolts evolved after the debut of *Uncle Tom's Cabin*. Harriet Stowe was an abolitionist who vexed disdain for impoverished slaves. She busted the perception that slaves were chattel, property, and had no Christian beliefs.

D.E.B. Dubois wrote that we Americans, both black and white, owe our gratitude for the freedom and the union that exist today in these United States. Upon the end of my syllabus, the professor crowned the Dubious debaters the victors.

Darting out of the building, a classmate pointed his fists at me and said he'll be back! I felt threatened and wanted justice on school turf. A human bulwark separated us, permitting him to get away. Body radar and high blood pressure signaled that my life was in danger. An impudent strafe was about to take place. A sophomore on a college campus, I courted the student lounge for battle. I waited for my next class sitting on a countertop close to exit doors and thirty yards from the cafeteria. The Gods had other plans for me.

In a flash, death was approaching me. Draped in a green military Jacket and shotgun barrels visible on his left shoulder bundled in a green blanket, he stood in front of me. Once the device began rotating from his shoulder, I unfettered a powerful left hook to his right jaw, stripping him of the weapon. As my eyes trailed the shotgun in the air, he drew a knife from his left pocket and stuck me in my stomach's right side. He withdrew the blade and tried twice to strike my chest. I was able to catch metal in the meaty part of my right arm. Unleashing another left hook, I whacked him to the floor. Frozen eyes were apparent. He did not forsee the punch delivery. I staggered to the shotgun, yanked off the wool, put the double barrel on his head, and set to fire the trigger, but there was no trigger guard. He vacated the scene. Law enforcement responded and educated me that if I would have squeezed the trigger, I would face first-degree murder charges because he was in a vulnerable state. I was no longer a victim, but transmuted into an assailant. This is Missouri law. Lifted in the medical transport, I was dashed to the city hospital notorious for mending puncture wounds.

Paramedics maneuvered my stretcher alongside a chain of bodies demanding the surgeon scalpel. I counted twelve patients with gun injuries. Objecting to being stagnated, I barked for medical assistance. A Chinese doctor roughly dug his finger in my flesh and said in English, "You would live!" Famous Barr duds save my life. A white and cold winter led me to the closet, choosing a thick sweater and a leather coat to wear. The combination of fleece and heavy rawhide averted a fatal calamity.

I got a flash on black crime that day. The criminal scourge is out of control. You can die because there is a shortage of doctors coping with canals of leaking blood in the streets. The white man is not the investigator of this fomentation.

What would Harriet Stowe think of free people today? How would she describe black on black crime? Enshrined in news vaults, the crux is rarely discussed. Eyes are wide shut and burn with hatred, charging racism every time a Caucasian slays a black person. Don't be blind; men of color slaughter white people as well! Afro-Americans must apprehend they do not have exclusive rights on slavery.

Jews, Indians, Mexicans, Hebrews, Romans, Serbs, Arabs, and Asians were all slaves at some decimal in history. Blacks are the only race still reacting to old history that you cannot mutate.

In St. Louis, Missouri, there is an area called the Central West End. A young white lady was jogging with a small infant in a stroller. Two black males robbed her and shot the baby when she held her purse. An *Empire* actor reported a fake story that Trump fans ambushed him. Black racists procure leniency from the media as white criminals are debased.

Not stating the facts only prevaricates additional untruths. I say to the millenniums, white citizens have made the sacrifice to make America great again. Several have lost their lives passing the torch to you.

Black millionaires who denounce America, I implore you this question: if this country is so racist, how did you become wealthy? You did not walk alone, achieving success. Pioneers before you laid the groundwork for your journey. Be real, America!

The controversy is anticipated with *Ungrateful Citizen*. Inciting the depiction was pure pleasure. I already made reservations to hop the best selling list with your patronage. It's only fair that black electors fervor President Trump for a 2020 win. My mission will be complete if voters carry *Ungrateful Citizen* in their thoughts, uniting this great land. We are the home of the brave, please do right and say, "I am grateful," America!

Years later, my school rival spotted me at a Little League football game. He introduced himself and apologized for the incident that occurred some time ago. In return, I accepted his peace treaty. I did not see him coming! He had changed, sporting a beard and a smaller frame. My anger had subsided after two years when my radar told me I was safe. His presence reaffirmed that my instincts were correct. The moral of this story is, be careful who you target; it can backfire!

6

———————

MURDER, INC.

CHAPTER SIX CONNOTES the mystery of body counts in America. Organized crime gets a fly this time around. I want to concentrate on abortion genocides, lone wolf hunters, mother nature disasters, serial killers, and suicides. Jointly these inequities shape Murder, Inc. to be liable for more deaths than military wars.

The supreme court ruled in ROE V. WADE that it was legal for women to exercise the right to abort babies in the United States. As a result, 100 million infants have been terminated. Genocides did not outdo this number in Cambodia, German concentration camps, Serbs, or Rwanda struggles. Frankenstein physicians were exposed in court for numerous barbarities.

Doctor Kermit Gosnell was convicted in 2013 for operating a clinic of horror. Cracking the backbone of infants, beheading babies with scissors, and providing an overdose of sedatives to a patient ended his evil deeds.

New York Doctor Robert Rho was hauled off to jail on May 16, 2016, for releasing a six months pregnant woman from his care with abortion complications. She later bled to death while being driven to the hospital.

Thirty-six fetuses from late-term abortions were discovered in the office of Doctor Nicola Irene. The court verdict was guilty as charged in Salt Lake City, Utah.

Doctor Steven Chase Brigham of Voorhee, New Jersey, was found guilty of five counts of manslaughter and practicing without a license.

In 1995m Doctor David Benjamin clipped a woman's uterus, causing her to bleed out during an abortion procedure.

Republicans proposed the born live abortion survivors protection act recently. Banishing abortions after the baby is conceived was the purpose, and punishing the doctors with prison tickets if they fail to comply. March 4, 2019, was the date Democrats denied and voted against the legislation. Fifty-three senators voted to back the bill. The other forty-four demurred a no vote.

The states of New York and Virginia are scouts in murdering babies. What proof does America need to protect the White House and the future of the kids? Controversy dictates the 2020 election, with President Trump caressing precious babies in pink and blue pajamas dangling little American flags. It would be clever to make this vision a television commercial for the 2020 run.

To the men of this gorgeous nation, I expect we are not associates in our bloodline's mass genocide. You owe the mother of your children forever grace for birthing your child. Halt mourning on child support payments and put a smile on your face that the mother of your child had the courage to bring part of you into this fabulous universe. Contraception must be left on the menu for men to reduce abortions in America. Medical czars try putting non-fertile drugs in glass bottles for men and women to absorb, preventing unwanted pregnancy. It's more humane this way.

Isolated in a world of personal grievances and political ideology wanders the hunter. He most likely developed his appetite for mayhem when he stepped on his first insect. Rapidly, he realized the prey was too small to satisfy the welcome savageness. Rabbits, squirrels, deer, turkey, and wild boars tantalize him more, but he is still unsatisfied. He lusts for bigger carnage and publicity. Prowling for attention from residents, it is his basic necessity to be recognized. The only quarry left on earth to please this diet for bloody murder scenes is people.

Highly intelligent, he plans to invade movie theaters, churches, public parks, schools, workplace environments, and beaches for mass annihilation without regrets. Typically letters, e-mail, manifestos, and photos are trickled behind, giving intentions to the rage. The government will tell you these incidents or rare by blood seekers. On record, there have been 2,500 petitions of this nature filed with the FBI. According to the vox tracker and gun violence archives, this data is one case too many, reflecting three thousand lives lost and four thousand wounded.

President Trump was on point again when quizzed about the New Zealand shooting attacker when he said a small number carry out such acts. Hate action is only two percent of the total murder rates. Homicides and suicides are higher. That translates to: American citizens are the most dangerous group in our society, not to the President of these United States. Take that race card and discard it now! You have no merit to cast foolish gossip or stones towards a stable president.

Proud of their openness, the hunter does not care if he dies or lives. He wants bragging rights for his signature moments. Huntsmen take pride in their kill of a bear, elephant, buffalo, or geese. Treasures are often displayed in homes, malls, or businesses. Mass massacres are posted over news cable. Families and society must be warned when the hunter is running loose. We, as a nation, must excrete and condemn the tracker perpetually. If we fail, they win—because they got away with merciless harm using bombs and military-style weapons.

Memorial flashbacks suckle the healing process for domestic and international enclaves.

- February 14, 2018 (17) people slain at the Marjory Stoneman Douglas High School in Parkland, Florida
- October 2017 (58) people murdered on Las Vegas strip
- In 2016 (49) people killed at gay night club in Orlando, Florida
- December 14, 2012, Sandy Hook Elementary savagery included (6) teachers and (20) children in Newton, Connecticut
- July 20, 2012, over (70) non-fatal injuries and (12) killed from bullets and grenades at an Aurora, Colorado Movie Theatre

The blueprint of the hunter: he or she slays unarmed people for recreation. Animals in the safari kill prey for a meal in order to exist. It's crystal clear they are wiser than people.

Murder rates are escalating within the States. Research from the FBI uniform crime report and the National Law Enforcement Fund and other data engines bases information on death certificates received from medical examiner sheets in each city and state. Numbers may be inaccurate due to errors in the system. A sample study will be explored for the years 2015, 2016, 2017, and 2019.

THE KING CITIES with high murder rates are St. Louis, Baltimore, Detroit, New Orleans, Birmingham, Jackson, Baton Rouge, Hartford, Salinas, and Milwaukee. Four states saw a jump in homicides in the year 1992.

Six-eight percent of murders in 1992; the weapons chosen were 55% firearms or 15% knives and cutting tools. 44% were killed by friends, 22% by strangers, 20% by family members, and senseless verbal altercations. For all groups, black males age 15-24 had the highest homicide rate of 159 per 100,000 population. The pattern is different for white men. They self destruct with 251,772 stressful suicides. This type of death befalls southern and westward regions of our country.

Arkansas, Alabama, Texas Mississippi led the South while New Mexico, Nevada, Colorado, and Arizona head the western states.

The federal Center for Disease Control and Prevention department claims police murdered 1,166 suspects averaging three deaths every twenty-four hours. Officers fallen in the line of duty reached 144 in 2018 and 129 in 2017. From 1980-2014, 64 cops were murdered per year. Michigan, Missouri, Indiana, and Illinois reported 84,113 homicides in 2008-2016.

Murder, Inc. is a killing machine in America, wouldn't you agree? We are a culture of vampires, famishing for the sight of blood. What are the motives for powering hatred to purloin individual life? See the six deuces of death and acknowledge that Murder, Inc. is a racist conglomerate executed by all ethnic groups, not just white heritage.

1. Jealousy
2. Revenge
3. Power
4. Money
5. Greed
6. Disputes

Serial killers indulge in a game of hide and seek. Often they provoke the law to snag them, obviating an uncontrollable tantrum to torture and maim victims.

FBI crime statistics report 15,000 murders per year. It is estimated less than 100 serial killers are operating in the confines of America and represent one percent of all murders performed in the states. The definition of a serial killer is anyone that murders three people in a year and plans a series of lone fatal abomination. Face tone totes shades of peacock feathers; anybody can become a member of Murder, Inc.

Three allegories of serial killers have spread for a decade. Many believe Caucasian men are sole serial killers. Don't be deceived; Asian, Latino, and African Americans are grounded in the melting pot. Hollywood made white serial killers movie stars. Unpopular with screenwriters, their competition earned a reputation on their own.

The "Railroad Killer," Rafael Ramires of Mexican descent killed (15) women and men in Illinois, Texas, and Kentucky.

Coral Watts, a black man in Michigan, murdered (17) women on Sunday by slashing each throat. Media wrote he was the "Sunday Morning Slasher."

Untamed in the city of Cleveland, the "Cleveland stranger" Abducted and mutilated (11) women in Ohio. His real name was Anthony Sowell.

The question lost in conversation is, are there any female serial killers? The answer is yes. Waiting for your inquiry in crime data files, you'll find 17 percent of serial homicides are women. This fact should not petrify the population. Females in the wild are skillful hunters. They have a legacy of mauling senior male lions in the den.

Going on a crime spree for long periods without capture is an indication the serial killer is bold and bright. He knows how to linger among us without detection. He could be a stranger, relative, friend, or work next to you. Specializing in the art of deception, he lays low until it's time to strike. Law enforcement on standby have outwitted these sociopaths. Their fate usually lands them in prison for long terms, execution by the government, or at the police's hands when resisting an arrest warrant. The evolution of notable killers spans 119 years, revoking Jack the Ripper traumatizing the white chapel district in London around 1888. Presently, Samuel Little confessed to 93 female casualties. The California court system convicted him on three counts of murder during 1987, 1988, and 1989.

Mother nature is the Godmother of all body figures on American loam. Her soldiers are busy at work, taking lives and destroying property, costing billions of dollars to rebuild a city or countryside. Scientists have granted the weather coterie destructive names. In the tropics, they are termed hurricanes, cyclones, typhoons, and tornadoes, which use powerful winds to ravish the heavens, land, and sea. Out west, wildfires and floods rip the low and highlands, leaving death everywhere. She then dresses for extreme hot and cold weather, canceling more lives from the earth.

Recovery terms reporting to natural disasters fail to find missing corpses. The world meteorological organization maintains charts on death documents in hazard storm systems.

For the sake of this Chapter, Region IV of North America was discussed. I cannot provide reasonable math for loss of life based on mother nature's rampage. She is the only wing of Murder, Inc. that eludes justice and retaliation for her malignant atrocities put on residents. A pretty rainbow cautions us that mother nature is asleep, constraining her violent pensive swings.

7

———————

OVERKILL

ON MARCH 24, 2019, the Mueller report was handed over to Attorney General William Barr for precis. In his summary, President Donald Trump did not collude with the Russian government in the 2016 election. Secondly, he did not obstruct justice in the matter. Upon hearing the brief, the President was bittersweet about the special council response! Some people expected him to jump up and down, laughing at the sore losing Democrats.

Staying presidential, he reacted with poise, ripping the report from its core. The feedback was justified after watching the Mueller probe sending his affiliates to jail. He knew full well if that he were found guilty of the two charges facing him, the summation would have been contrary to today's decision.

As a citizen, I foresaw this day approaching when I stroked the first letter of the *Ungrateful Citizen*. Frozen eyes and mental shock by Democrats unfurled across the nation. Swallowing Alka-Seltzer or dropping a cocktail couldn't inundate the agony of defeat once again. The Senate intelligence arrived at the same conclusion when they completed their investigation on February 7, 2019.

Unable to trust the verdict, the Democratic Party insists on overthrowing the White House with stale pretensions and rowdy tactics entreating the full report; a typical reaction from a beaten adversary.

Smoke signals of rebellion have reorganized the Republicans to track facts disguised in Fisa Court and Dossier Forms: I implore Senator Lindsey Graham and the Senate to uncover plots to assassinate President Trump before and after the 2020 election. Trail this path, and you will trace the sponsor back to the previous administration.

I just provided you with a common sense tip why the intel community did not tell President Trump of the danger circling him and his family. Assassination was the final option on the table to regain the oval office. Once the plots are identified, Marines dressed in blues must make executive arrests on artificial heads mounted on spikes for high treason. The exposition must be seen at world museums, echoing the Trump coup faltered.

JOHN

BRENNAN

ADAM

SCHIFF

JERROLD

NADLER

JAMES

COMEY

AMERICA. Do not desert your President. The 2020 Ballot Box will define our past and future. Do you pose with the leader or not? It's plain logic. Why did the losing party spend over 40 million dollars to chase Trump from work? There is one reason! He is the right person occupying the throne at this time in history. It's not about what the President can do for you, but will the nation prop a brave and witty President?

Pitching mud at Trump's personal attorney for hours over a three-day stretch was grimly and pitiless. Showing total disregard for attorney-client privilege, he sang like a yellow canary to the Democratic Party's donkey ears. Relying on a monologue from a lawyer in transit to prison is absurd and unfair.

Screening mob films, Congress tried to duplicate court affidavits where guilty pawns took down their boss. Squeaking, they ordered them to defect. Unlawful crimes: Michael Cohen cannot be the judge, jury, and executioner of the President. Neither can Congress. The President must receive a fair and intrinsic investigation of charges brought forth by the mule pack.

I have sought attorney work in my lifetime. Never did I place concern about his activities. I trusted him and was paying money for his help. Court records are proof that some attorneys are crooks. They steal from clients and sell them out to prosecutors. This is a diamond case whereby the President's word vetoes the attorney's version of their relationship. Cohen was found guilty of perjury and fraud. Noted as the fixer, he lacked the expertise to rescue himself from the stranglehold of Congress.

Sensors of the President pressed him to gather the best legal minds available to combat the Mueller manhunt. Upon introducing the dream team, America downloaded strong-arm tactics used by law enforcement to fool Trump's inner pool into asserting false statements unseating a newly elected President. There is no ambiguity in my mind the past administration apprised that Trump did not collude or obstruct justice with the Russians. He was a long shot at winning the election—nobody gave him a chance, including the Russians.

To justify their trickery, judges sentenced loyalists to jail and the FBI raided their homes and businesses. The media, Democrats, and liberals did not consider the nation, and I myself observed political spectators not handling losing the 2016 elections nobly. As repeated in this opus, the mental shock and frozen eyes description strengthens that the nemesis is stuck on stupid!

Attorney Jay Sekulow and Rudolph W. Giuliani earn high praise for loyalty to the President. Listening to the news pounding untrue babbling—employees leaving the White House was just another outrageous delusion.

On the heels of the Mueller findings, the President has no chance but to pardon Manafort and stone for jail time received. Digging in their background was a cover-up concealing; there was no linkage between Russia and the President.

To the shaky Republicans who deluded Trump, I say to you: your Democratic underwear has no value. You are on the list for disloyalty to our President. Your names are on scrolls in a torn Congress. Senator John McCain departed too soon. He leaked the dossier to the public, wrote a book defaming the President, and did the thumb down on his health care proposal. All this drama from a man who had prior notice he was going to die. May you rest in peace: the President outlasted you and frivolous Democrats.

To sum up, things the government impaled, a game of "overkill" to nullify the 2016 election results. After forty million dollars wasted, the recap was surreal. President Trump has been exonerated for all to gravitate. The rally in Michigan is a testament he put fun and passion in the political campaign. His enthusiasm is breathtaking and delightful. Prolonging misery, only the ungrateful citizen can erode this victorious momentum with tender feelings. So what, you get offended when you hear words you do not appreciate! I recommend you take aspirin to reduce your unwell stress—President Trump will lift his hands again in 2020.

Easter Sunday is high, and as usual, the world is prepared to celebrate His resurrection. It is the best day of the year; I am free to partake with kids on Easter egg hunts, crunching jelly beans, and rabbit chocolates, not to mention the scent of ham, potato salad, and rolls.

Blessing the food was mandatory in our household before raking the mouth. This year would be resuscitating for me, believing Jesus rose from the dead. The twelve apostles were the social media annotating Jesus' revival was real. For their missions of instilling faith in Christianity, the saints met deplorable executions. Conjecture crept into my skull, Rome had the mentality of the Mueller search to decimate innocent lives obscuring the truth.

- Judas hung himself after betraying Jesus.
- Matthias traveled to Syria and was put to death by fire.
- James clubbed and stoned to death in Syria.
- Thomas died from a spear assault from ancient Marthoma soldiers.
- Andrew was crucified in Greece.
- Matthew was stabbed to death in Ethiopia.
- Paul was beheaded around 66 AD during the reign of Roman Emperor Nero.
- Peter crucified upside down because he believed he was not worthy of death in the same manner as Jesus.
- Simon was killed for not sacrificing to the Sun God.
- John escaped boiling oil in Rome and wrote the last book of revelation in the New Testament. He also took care of Mary, the mother of Jesus, when she visited his home.
- Bartholomew's death is unclear. There are no accurate stories of how he was slain.
- Phillip was tortured for exposing Roman proconsul's wife to Christianity.

Sharing this wonderment with you was enlivening; churches do not speak of the Apostles' butcheries. In the Western world, fame has been paid to Jesus' disciples. Their first names are common for males born.

In her glory days, Rome cloned the science of "Overkill," and it did not stop Christianity from strewing all over the world. I come back to mount cavalry on this Sunday. Do not forsake President Trump in the 2020 elections. Dark days will ensue, teasing World War III if you repudiate Trump as President of these United States of America.

8

AMERICAN DREAM

BASEBALL HERO BOB GIBSON gracefully sowed seeds of the American Dream when he uttered a vaunted reminiscence. I was here for a long time. I'm proud to say I've seen a lot of changes. Things are altogether different than they were in 1959, and I mean all for the better.

Decisively a sturdy citizen, has elucidated memories of the past. Four blocks of Bob Gibson way in St. Louis, MO is too short. Natural Bridge Boulevard ranging from downtown to the airport, could have been renamed Bob Gibson Way. In my second year of high school, I noticed Big Bob Gibson falling off the mound pitching baseball's Cardinals to another World Series in 1967. He was so impressive the Major League lowered the hill contesting his influential expo. It was too late for a blackout! Youth were energized to befit pitching positions. I was one of them, and struggled with the curveball on full-count throws. Coaching clinics would have helped my imperfection to benefit Vashon baseball contests. In the early sixties, Fundamental Academies were uncommon in black districts.

Ablaze in my spirits is the thrill to pursue images of composing books. When I first learned that slaves were not given the freedom to read and dealt death if caught writing, I pledged to illuminate the world on its political woes. *Big*, *We Can Do More*, and *Ungrateful Citizen* are my gems thus far. Cogitating a promise kept to repel old slave codes, I looked to the cosmos.

Knowledge is power and it frightened slave owners to post restrictions, making it a crime to teach both the freed and still enslaved the skills to write and read. Slave code in theory and practice outlawed charrettes in the States of Virginia 1819 and South Carolina 1740. Twenty lashes were the penalty for violations at any courthouse.

In South Carolina, any person teaching slaves forfeit the sum of one hundred pounds in punitive damages.

Overlooking slave statutes, bondservants taught themselves to read and write. This tradition resides worldwide captivating authors, like myself, who are ready and willing to balance rival aspects.

The entrepreneur's fire did not end with me, but is propelled throughout men wearing business suits. They were wealthy magnates and philanthropists who erected this country.

John Pierpont Morgan Sr. instituted the House of Morgan from 1837-1913. He understood that whoever hegemonize the financial system had the power over their competitors in the business world. The Morgan Banking Dynasty gobbled U.S. steel, General Electric, and the railroads, because agents of each empire defaulted on bank loans and were unable to pay court fees to settle disputation.

John D. Rockefeller Sr. was an industrialist who uncovered and refined oil to make plastic products. He also invented kerosene lamps, competing with Thomas Edison and J.P. Morgan for lighting up homes, cars, and roads in America.

Cornelius Vanderbilt had a monopoly on railroad freight for 100 years, launching in 1820. Union Pacific and Central Pacific railroad linked the East and West coasts in Omaha, Nebraska. This rail challenge was completed in only six years, from 1863-1869. Traveling by train, Amtrak passenger cars yielded and let freight boxes on the tracks. In 1832, Matthias Bald engineered the first locomotives. Speed for these iron horses was 30 miles per hour, shortening a six month trip to just six days.

Henry Ford designed the assembly line technique to mass-produce automobiles. Racing cars convicted investors to market his Model T Ford in 1910. Cars were abundant around 1900, encouraging cities to append more roads and highways.

Andrew Carnegie ruled the steel industry for a long time providing steel tracks for the railroad. Labor battles shut down plants, causing massive layoffs. Bitter because he lost his job, Leon Czolgosz shot President McKinley in 1901. Under new leadership, steel rebounded —with tall skyscrapers in towns and bridges leaning across waterways.

World War I recorded military generals ordering trucks to move troops in combat zones for four years, 1914-1918. Companies adjoined trucks to their assembly lines after the war to transport bulky loads.

Chicago held a meeting in 1933, calling for industries to comply with the code of fire competition. Ted Rodgers was appointed the first President of American Highway Freight. The Motor Carrier Act of 1935 regulated the truck industry. Trucks shipped commodities faster than trains, holding prices to lower rates. Transporting livestock of pork, beef, sheep, turkey, chicken, and refrigerated crops enfeebled the train giant.

Man-made canals were dug to maintain low costs for maritime freight transportation aboard cargo ships. Cruise ships provided vacation tours for people, and other boats were used in military, recreation, and sports tournaments. The boating industry has been around since 1787, unlocking steamboats, rafts, and flatboats floating down river channels.

The Civil Aeronautics Board engendered the Air Traffic System and airline deregulations. Planes became a major player in commerce, both locally and abroad.

Homes emerged from the wood economy in 1540. Timber trade, logging, and forestry supplied furniture, wood, pulp, and energy firms.

Adam Smith's book, *The Wealth of Nations,* published in 1776, portrays the automation and technology ideas relayed in this chapter. He harbored the Laissez Faire Principle—that the government should not interfere in private business transactions, and that people held an "invisible hand" of self-motivation to earn money, contributing to a blooming economy. Mr. Smith expressed that labor gave products their value, and understanding that premise set up the upsurge inside labor unions to fight for a fair share of cash profited by striking, disrupting the flow of items to the public.

Freedom rings in America, and we have the moral imperative to censure socialism cushioning our lifestyle as we know it. My home is not beholden to cries for slave reparations. Conquered people relinquish such rights on bloody battlegrounds. America has compromised better living conditions for its citizens. The jumble of the far left is provoking civil war and flustering discontent with their detached tongues. A vote for Trump on November 3, 2020, will avert possible bloodshed.

The Democrats' Green New Deal is nothing more than a mirage addressing climate change. Man will flop seducing and controlling mother nature. This is God's work; once man attempted to raise a tower pointed to the heavens. God did not assent this imagination and disciplined the workers with different languages so that they could not communicate as one think tank—stopping the chimera from trespassing the grounds of heaven.

On March 27, 2019, the Senate rejected the Green New Deal and its reforms. Replacing fossil fuels completely and reducing carbon emissions in 10 years was the root message. Dismantling the transportation and agriculture systems were a second goal. Thirdly, directing the government to finance lazy residents with free money and jobs is unrealistic.

The colonies rebelled against England over a similar rationale. America is the master of all revolutions. She will not embrace Blacks, Arabs, Indians, or any other diversity group exploiting the U.S. Constitution. Your lives will be changed for the worse. Consider the Middle East and Central America incubus.

President Franklin D. Roosevelt is the genius beyond the New Deal— the public work projects, economics, and social reforms that uplifted America out of the great depression. Suffering lasted for ten years, from October 1929 to 1939. Rep. Alexandria Cortez stole his thunder when she inaugurated the Green New Deal on February 7, 2019.

Open your eyes, America, and concede President Trump's economic policy is the envy of the world. I have come to accept that the Democrats not only despise Trump, but jiggle in jealousy of his vogue leading this preeminent nation. Candidates in a bubble are human piranhas, fascinated by the Trump mystic and want only to take his place for self-glory. Is this what you want, America?

THE END.

ABOUT THE AUTHOR

Born in Memphis, Tennessee, Gene Earl Bradford has composed three books: Big, We Can Do More, and Ungrateful Citizen. Ungrateful Citizen is his newest release, reminding the nation to remain focused on the upcoming election in 2020.

The skills to create the above works were learned in the printing department at O'Fallon Technical High School in St. Louis, Missouri, from 1965 to 1969. Bradford graduated with an associate's degree in law enforcement from Forest Park Community College and finished his final two years with a bachelor of science degree at the University of Missouri-St. Louis

A Vietnam veteran, Bradford executed missions in Yankee Station Theatre and was a personal bodyguard and orderly aboard the U.S.S. Coral Sea (CVA-43). At the time of publication, Bradford has been retired for 18 months from the U.S. Postal Service after a tenure of 36 years. He retired as a proud union member and a member of the National Association of Letter Carriers, Branch 343.

Bradford was inducted in Mathews-Dickey Boys' and Girls' Club Hall of Fame for organizing the MDBC Kiddie Patrol, who was in place at the Club Grand Opening in 2002. In addition, he coached a Little League powerhouse football team to six Super Bowl Championships and three national titles in the states of Florida and Georgia.

www.ingramcontent.com/pod-product-compliance
Lightning Source LLC
Chambersburg PA
CBHW061732250726
48657CB00002B/882

9798554064128